WHOSE CAT ARE YOU?
Front and Back Covers

Valerie Singleton (see page 8)

Ruth Rendell (see page 14)

Lady Fairbairn (see page 28)

Francis King (see page 18)

Was That the Fridge Door? Etching by Susie Perring

WHOSE CAT ARE YOU?

Some Famous People and their Cats

by Nicholas Reed

This book illustrates and describes the cats of fifteen celebrities. We are grateful to them all for participating in this book. Among them are an actress, a TV presenter, several novelists, an artist, a distinguished historian, and two campaigners for animals.

The descriptions of their cats are all given in their own words, though some are the result of interviews we made with them. The final chapter gives brief details of the cats of over twenty other celebrities (including two royal cats).

PS A learned academic footnote, in suitably small print, for those who like that sort of thing:

About two hundred years ago, the poet Alexander Pope had a dog collar made for a dog which he then gave to Frederick Prince of Wales (later King George II). On the collar was inscribed:

"I am His Highness' dog at Kew;
Pray tell me, Sir, Whose dog are you?"

Published in 1994 by

Lilburne Press,
26 Hichisson Road
London SE15 3AL

First edition 1994
© Nicholas Reed

ISBN 0 9515258 8 3

CONTENTS

VALERIE SINGLETON

Valerie Singleton is probably still best remembered, to a certain youthful generation, as one of the presenters of the children's programme Blue Peter, *from 1962 to 1972. On that programme, the three presenters were always accompanied by both a cat and a dog when they were introducing features. But Valerie is also remembered for the* Blue Peter Royal Safari, *in which she accompanied Princess Anne, now the Princess Royal, on the Princess's first tour abroad as President of the Save the Children Fund. Valerie went on to make four series of* Blue Peter Special Assignment, *which took her round the world. But her achievements with* Blue Peter *should not blind us to the varied and distinguished career she has had since then. In 1972, she moved to present TV's* Nationwide, *and then in 1978 to* Tonight. *During most of the 1980s she was a presenter on* The Money Programme, *as well as a host of Radio 4's* PM, *while in 1994 she became a presenter on the TV programme* Next.

My two cats are sisters: Pansy, a tortoiseshell, and Daisy, a tabby. Both have now reached respectable middle-age, but are still very lively. I acquired them from a friend of mine when they were still kittens. Pansy was the "runt" of the litter, but has turned out to be a smashing little cat: very friendly, and a real clown. She's always waiting at the top of the stairs to greet me when I get back.

Curiously, she did not learn to miaow until she was about eight: first, as a little squeak as greeting, then eventually deciding her voice was quite respectable at normal volume. She is also highly intelligent: knows just what I mean when I ask what she can see down below, when sitting at the bathroom window. She also understands what "No" means, without any need to push the point further.

Daisy is a very affectionate cat, but rather more nervous: she needs persuading to come on my lap, while Pansy will leap on at the slightest excuse. Pansy likes being "blow-waved" with the hair dryer: especially if it is put on "cold" in the hot weather. Daisy, meanwhile, prefers to be vacuumed: it presumably cleans deep down where it matters!

JOSIE LAWRENCE

Josie Lawrence started as a straight actress, but some sketches at the Comedy Store Players (where she still appears), followed by frequent appearances on Channel 4's Whose Line is it Anyway? *established her as a brilliant comedian. A recent achievement on TV was to extemporise a love-duet featuring a cat litter tray, and featuring the immortal refrain, "Let's litter our lives with love." What next?*

I have two tomcats: Anoch and Ayli. I suppose their names are really Enoch and Eli, but where I came from: the Black Country in the West Midlands, Anoch and Ayli are the two stock characters used in cartoons or jokes. I first spotted Anoch as an eight-week-old kitten in a garden full of cats, looked after by a lady from the Cats' Protection League. All his brother and sister kittens had been adopted, but he was left, simply because he was long-haired! Soon after I took him, I felt he needed a pal, so when I heard of another kitten being left alone in a small bedsit, another rescue seemed appropriate.

When Ayli was delivered at my front door, I felt this black and white cat was really ugly, and such a contrast to handsome Anoch! In fact, Ayli's ears were so large that, if you held his photo upside-down, he looked more like a fruit-bat! After the initial stand-off period, both cats have become great friends and now always sleep together on my bed. Now I know them better, Anoch can be described as handsome but dim; Ayli is less handsome, but much cleverer. You've probably seen film of cats opening a door by turning the handle? My two do a double-act: Ayli pushes the handle down, while Anoch pushes the door open! Ayli's special tipple is asparagus; Anoch's favourite activity is washing me. Their other pet occupation is catching a goldfish from the neighbour's pond and depositing it at my feet. The nice thing is that the fish is always alive, so after popping it in water, I can take it back to the neighbours. I had my birthday recently (D-day: 6th of June), and my cats duly brought me a goldfish as a present: how thoughtful of them!

Opposite: Josie Lawrence with Anoch. (Photo: Scope Features)

SIR ROY STRONG

Sir Roy Strong is probably best-known as the former director of the Victoria and Albert Museum. But more recently he has published further work on Tudor Portraiture, and on gardens generally, including a series on television. He has been closely involved in the proposed reconstruction of the 18th century gardens at Hampton Court Palace.

Larkin and Souci are American Maine Coons, two years old. They are already enormous large-limbed creatures, but we understand that they really begin to fill-out in year three, ending up like little mobile sofas. They are long-haired and some would describe them more as tails with cats attached, but they are very beautiful: Larkin a silver tabby, and Souci, tabby and white. They are the successors of a much loved common moggie called the Reverend Wenceslas Muff, who now rests beneath a gilded ball in the garden.

Larkin is named after a Jacobean painter called William Larkin whose works I recently catalogued, and Souci commemorates a visit to San Souci, Frederick the Great's palace outside Berlin. In fact his full name is Herzog Friedrich von Sans Souci, but I regret to say he gets called "Souse".

As we lost Muff through feline Aids (FIV), these beloved creatures are house cats, but with a large exterior pen in which to climb, sprawl and take the air. Once a day they have their harnesses put on for a walk around the garden. Although half-brothers, they have little similarity in character. Larkin is timid and highly strung, rather hung-up as a cat in fact, dignified and angular in his movements, asking for affection only when he needs it, when he stretches up and asks to be picked up and hugged. Souci is a loose-limbed, hanging out all over the place kind of cat: a wayward bundle of love who cheerfully chirrups his way through life. Larkin sits bolt upright in my arms, while Souci drapes himself around my upper half like a scarf. We couldn't live without them.

Sir Roy Strong holding Larkin, with his wife Julia Trevelyan Oman holding Souci.

A double portrait of Sir Roy by Paul Brason, with the Rev Wenceslas Muff lying low. Exhibited at the Royal Academy in 1988.

RUTH RENDELL

Ruth Rendell and PD James are frequently bracketed together as our two most distinguished thriller writers, though PD James is more strictly a writer of detective novels. Ruth Rendell's first thriller was published in 1964, since when she has produced at least one book a year. Her books have been translated into seventeen languages; six have so far have been adapted for television, and two made into films. The two most recent TV adaptations, Gallowglass *and* A Fatal Inversion, *were repeated in summer 1994, while a new series of TV adaptations started in September 1994. In addition, she has written* Ruth Rendell's Suffolk: the county in which she lives. *In her private life she is a vegetarian, which she says she was conditioned to "by the knowledge of what was happening to animals, stuffed with hormones and steroids".*

A month ago I could have said I had four cats but then our poor Percy died, to our sorrow and, I regret to say, the great delight of the remaining three. He was a mild, gentle and handsome cat but for some reason they all hated him.

Now I have Sukey the old tabby, aged about 15 but looking much younger and hunting like a kitten; Blanche, she of the snow and marmalade coat and paws full of sharp pins frequently used; and Bunbury the Blue Cat, small, neat, intelligent and with something near a sense of humour. I did not name Blanche after Blanche Dubois, but they have a lot in common.

I have no space here to write about them all, so Bun it must be. He is our only affectionate cat - Blanche is passionate, not the same thing - and the only one that enjoys being cuddled. He loves warmth, sleeps on the shelf beside the Aga summer and winter or snuggled in the airing cupboard. When bored on long winter evenings he will go up to each sleeping lady cat and give her a swipe so that she wakes up in a rage and chases him round the house, roaring curses at him. He hunts hornets, catches and eats them. He likes to hide and then appear nonchalantly when you have started to worry. Bun is a rich slate-blue with a white vest and paws, silver whiskers and lime-green eyes.

Opposite: Ruth Rendell with Bunbury

CELIA FREMLIN

Celia Fremlin is the author of many suspense novels, the first being The Hours before Dawn; *the latest,* Listening in the Dark. *Her novels have many of the psychological and suspense features of those by Ruth Rendell, and some people prefer them, as they can be less "grim" than Ms Rendell's. Celia's books are even more popular in Germany than they are here: two having been adapted for German TV. Her books have been translated into seventeen languages: by coincidence, this is exactly the same number as those by Ruth Rendell.*

My previous cat, Caractacus, was a lively ginger tom, who once appeared briefly on TV, having jumped on my lap during an interview. He was a rescue, and was extremely nervous when he first came here. However, when shown the cat door, he sussed it out immediately: it seems his previous owners must have had one!

Our present cat Stripey came to me as a three-year-old, and is now nearly seven. He was actually given to my daughter, who already had two cats, so I agreed to take him on. We did try to give him a more interesting name: Sir Scudamore, after the gentle parfit knight of Spenser's 'Fairie Queen'. But that name never stuck.

My husband Leslie and I always sit down to watch the six o'clock news. It is presaged by the closing bars of "Neighbours", and as soon as this resounds round the house, Stripey always appears behind our chairs, ready to leap into a lap for half an hour of uninterrupted bliss!

Opposite: Celia Fremlin with Stripey (and rhinoceros)

FRANCIS KING

Francis King has written over twenty novels, as well as non-fiction works such as Florence *and* E M Forster and His World. *He most recently produced an autobiography, entitled* Yesterday Came Suddenly, *filled with reminiscences of some of the numerous writers and actors he has met, and appears with his Siamese cat on the front cover of the book. He is also a former President of the International Writers' Group PEN.*

I often describe her as a foundling. But in fact she found me, not I her. At the time my beloved Siamese cat, Louche, was nearing the close of her life. Every morning, outside my kitchen window, I would see this beautifully sleek long-haired black cat, with a red velvet collar round her neck. Every morning I would put out a plate of cat-food for her. She never attempted to enter the house through the cat-door.

Then Louche died. On the same day, I heard the cat-door bang. My daily visitor had clearly heard that the position of resident cat was soon to become vacant in my house and had decided to be the first to apply for it. I put up notices to say that a stray cat was with me, but, mysteriously, no-one ever claimed her.

At first, so thick was her coat, I assumed her to be a tom, and since my name is King, I called her Prince. I took her to the vet for her to be 'fixed'. The vet examined her and then roared with laughter. "This isn't Prince; this is Princess," she said. Princess she has remained.

I have no idea how old she is. But she has now been with me for almost twelve years and she is still agile enough to bring me - early in the morning, when I am still in bed - the far from welcome offering of a bird.

CARLA LANE

Carla Lane has written numerous comedies for TV, including The Liver Birds, Butterflies, The Mistress, *and* Bread. *Whilst continuing her writing, she also now helps to run* Animaline, *which "fights for the Peace and Dignity of all Animals". Its address is Broadhurst Manor, Horsted Keynes, near Haywards Heath, Sussex RH17 7BG. Telephone: 0342 810596.*

The head of my cat family is Wolfgang, a ginger tom, who gets his name because he is strong and stroppy - while still happy to welcome all new cats to the gang. Mia, a pure tabby, gets her name from the meer-cats which featured in a TV documentary made by David Attenborough. She is a real loner, and attacks all others. Pandora, so-called because of her changeable moods, is black on top and white underneath, and is much the most purry of the cats. Daniel, a pure tabby, is the most communicative, with the loudest voice: skilfully imitated by the parrot! He is the feline vacuum-cleaner, devouring everything offered, and a few other things besides, such as toast or sandwiches.

Irena, a very pretty feminine longhaired tabby, is happy to play by herself. Caspar, a big grey male, is a distinctly posh cat: hence his posh name. Lastly Sorrow, black with a finger of white, is the most mysterious of all my cats. I felt sorry for her, because my first sight of her as a wild cat was when she was being dragged out from under a pavement by workmen in Kensington, as I was walking past. She would have been put down had I not rescued her, so as my very first cat, she is very dear to me.

All my cats love avocado, as well as fresh cream. I know people say you shouldn't give them cream, but three of my cats are now over 15, and it doesn't seem to have done them the slightest harm.

Opposite: Carla Lane with, starting from the left, Pandora and Mia, Wolfgang in front, Sorrow behind him, and Irena in the distance. (Photo: Scope Features)

MOLLY HARDWICK

Molly Hardwick has spent much of her life as a writer and producer for radio drama. She also wrote the book adaptations (and novels) of The Duchess of Duke Street, Upstairs Downstairs, Juliet Bravo *and* By the Sword Divided. *With her husband, the late Michael Hardwick, she wrote several definitive works on Sherlock Holmes, Conan Doyle and Charles Dickens. But she would most like to be remembered for her biography of* Emma, Lady Hamilton *(1969), and for her Doran Fairweather mystery novels, of which the latest is* The Dreaming Damozel.

When my husband Michael died in 1991 I felt I must have a cat companion. Fenna, short for Fenella, came to me from a cat sanctuary in Ashford, Kent, when she was four months old. Bursting out from the sanctuary's cat-basket like a sunbeam in all her tortoise-shell beauty, she celebrated her release by running round the company assembled to welcome her, and snatched a portion of parkin from everybody's plate. Her charms were such that when I put the house on the market, the estate agent photographed her in the drawing-room, because he felt that the presence of such a cat added 'tone' to the advertisement.

She was a wild kitten, almost irrepressible. I tried to keep her in until she had been innoculated and spayed, but she escaped through a window with incredible acrobatic skill, and horrified all by making her way up the High Street along the peaks of the ancient roofs: and did it again and again.

But she soon realised she'd found her home. At first she always bolted her food down. Then one day she looked round carefully, ate her breakfast in a more leisurely manner, then looked up at me with happy understanding that this was Her Place - she no longer had to compete with eight other cats!

At four, she is no longer a wild child, but a calm, rather prim and Jane Austenian young lady, a creature of habit with an invisible little watch. In the evening I only need to call "Bed and Bikkies, Fenna", and she immediately appears from wherever she is and goes to settle on the bed upstairs, waiting for me to join her. She is home, with the complete freedom of the little London house and the garden with squirrels, and she shares it equally with me, her best friend as she is mine.

Opposite: Molly Hardwick with Fenna. The oval picture above is a contemporary portrait of Emma, Lady Hamilton.

RICHARD BAWDEN

The Suffolk-based artist Richard Bawden frequently uses cats as the subject or background for his paintings or prints; he has also designed a rather ingenious metal garden seat made out of cat designs. His father, Edward Bawden, the distinguished war artist and landscapist, also occasionally featured a cat in his paintings.

My cat Jester is now 17 years old. She is the product of a pedigree Siamese and a ginger tom whose passions apparently overruled his care for the importance of pedigree. Jester thus has a rather mottled coat, which earns her the nickname of "fruit cake". She loves to sleep in our bed, but is not allowed to do so till seven in the morning when she is permitted to enter to warm herself up.

She is clearly highly intelligent, and tends to growl at my mother-in-law: she certainly did so on the occasion when she said, "Perhaps it is about time we got you put down". She loves to sit on people's laps on appropriate occasions, such as if we are sitting down talking on the phone, or on less appropriate occasions, such as if one of us is sitting on the loo!

My previous cat "Winkle" was the product of an Abyssinian and a ginger tom (yes, you've guessed it: the same ginger tom). He died a year ago, but appears in some of my prints.

My father had several cats: one was Emma Nelson (compare Molly Hardwick elsewhere in this book), and one was "Tousy": short for Toulouse-Lautrec. He got that name because he was such an intellectual cat.

Opposite: two watercolours by Richard Bawden, who also produced The Cats' Christmas. *Above: Jester (centre-stage) and Tinker (a visitor) survey the scene in Richard's dining-room. Below:* Richard's Sitting-Room. *The keen-eyed may like to make comparisons with the sitting-room in* The Cats' Christmas!

BUNNY CAMPIONE

Bunny Campione has been appearing regularly on The Antiques Roadshow *for the last nine years, and, from the summer of 1994, on* The Great Antiques Hunt. *Her particular expertise is toys and teddybears.*

Originally we had two Burmese, Sultan and his brother Kaliph. Sadly, Kaliph was run over, so now Mishka is a rather nervous replacement. Sultan is a Lilac Burmese: I can only imagine they are called "lilac" because their ears are a little pink when the light is behind them. Otherwise they are cream with beige markings. Mishka is a blue Burmese. I have had Siamese and Burmese and moggies; but I have to say I prefer Burmese because they are slightly less neurotic than Siamese in general. One Burmese I had was left for two days in a room by mistake. Instead of dirtying the floor or bed or whatever, he did his business in the plughole of the basin! What incredible animals they are.

Why "Sultan"? Because it is a grand name for a grand cat. Sultan has lived with us now for five years: we bought him through a Burmese cat breeder. Sometimes we think he should be called "Floppy", as he flops about in front of you like a dog, and rolls on the back. If you then ignore him, he catches you round the ankles (though carefully keeping his claws in).

He adores getting under the bath mat and hiding; then he forgets and falls asleep, with just a paw sticking out. He always accompanies me and sits on the side of the bath when I'm in it. He will jump on my shoulders, which is fine if I'm dressed, but fairly excruciating if I'm not! Then he likes to travel around with his front legs on one shoulder, and hind legs straddling the other shoulder: rather like a lion on a tree!

He loves sleeping with anyone, but particularly my sons. He has to have his head as near to your cheek as possible, preferably with his whiskers tickling your face! He refuses to drink water from his bowl. Rather, he likes the bidet filled for him, and failing that, he will lick the watertap instead. He is a great football-player - the ball being a rolled-up piece of tinfoil. He will pat the ball all over the place, and then bring it back to you in his mouth, and drop it at your feet, ready for more.

Opposite: Sultan stands regally on his vantage point next to Bunny. They are standing behind what Bunny regards as her loveliest antique: a 16th century birdcage, probably from a French monastery. (Photo: Gary Moyes)

LADY FAIRBAIRN

*Lady Fairbairn is the wife of Sir Nicholas Fairbairn, QC, MP.
Sir Nicholas has been an MP for twenty years, and was Solicitor-
General for Scotland from 1979-82. They and their six cats live
in Fordell Castle in Fife, Scotland.*

I came home from attending to my husband in the House of Commons, at the State Opening of Parliament, to find my newest, most loved cat "Rug Pussy", who was black and white and came from the Cats Protection League in Spalding, had been killed in a snare. I immediately bought a small apricot-coloured Persian called "Colonel Chinstrap".

The Colonel is a remarkable person. His face is flat, as if he had run into a wall at great speed. He has the proper Poonah look, that Colonels ought to and used to have. He has a fully grown white moustache, which I have never seen before. In addition to his proud Colonel's whiskers, he has white boots and a spinnaker tail, like Squirrel Nutkin.

He spends most of the day sitting on the front doorstep guarding the Castle. The Colonel has one failure: he sleeps close to us every night. He purrs and snores and we cannot find the "switch-off" button.

I also have four wonderful Birmans, and a Moggy called Clive, and they all receive the same love and attention.

*Opposite: Lady Fairbairn with Colonel Chinstrap in their home Fordell
Castle. (Photo: Evening Standard)*

ERNA NAUGHTON

Erna Naughton is the widow of Bill Naughton, best remembered as the author of Alfie *(the novel was recently reissued by Allison and Busby), and the plays* Derby Day *and* Spring and Port Wine *(both revived in the theatre in 1994). On receiving two cat books from John Montgomery in 1968, Bill wrote, "I think that cats don't even yield on the printed page (self-sufficient sods), but you get close to making them." Bill and Erna Naughton moved in that year to the Isle of Man, and it was there that Bill died in 1992, at the age of 81.*

It was in March 1987, a rainy, cold and windy Manx evening, the light fading, when, standing at the window, I was aware of movement under some shrubs -- two little eyes shining out. Living near farms and knowing the animal husbandry does not include cats, and already having four stray Manx cats, I am well prepared for emergencies. I made up a dish with the best I could find, took it out, but as soon as he saw me he went further under the shrubs, though he kept his eyes more on the dish than on me.

I left the dish in a dry place and came back in, turned off the lights and could see him eating fast, looking round him in case it might be taken away from him. This went on ten evenings, while slowly I kept putting the food nearer the cat door. He watched me and would not eat while I was there: I had to be behind the window and he was safe. Because it was St Patrick's Day I started to call him Paddy. One day he let me touch him; he raised his little tail, all twisted, and slowly, feeling no danger, came into the house. He looked so small compared to the others, who stared at him. No-one raised a paw; he looked round, picked the cosiest place in the Cats' Parlour, and settled for the night. Slowly his mottled brown coat took on a shine and he put on weight. I said to my husband, "Isn't it lovely what a few weeks' food and a warm home did for him?"

One morning he was restless, and didn't touch his food. I had to go out. When I came back my husband told me he had something to show me; took me into where Paddy slept, and there he was, the happy mother of two kittens, looking up at me as if to say, "Did I surprise you?" She was a gentle and caring Mum. Often, to get away from her little family, she would jump on Bill's desk and, when his pen went too fast, would put her little paw on his hand to be let out. When, in 1991, Bill suffered a stroke, she got on his bed and licked his hand, cuddled beside him and purred. As Bill said, "It was like a little song for him." Now, over two years after Bill's death, Paddy still gets up on the desk and plays with pens left there.

Only death can teach us the true blessing of life.

The Naughtons with two earlier cats: Erna with Timmy Taylor, and Bill Naughton with Bobby.
Both cats originally came from England and so, unlike Manx cats, they did have tails!

VICTORIA MOORE

Victoria Moore is Chairman of Fight Against Animal Cruelty in Europe. *Established in 1987, it now has 100 members (address: 29 Shakespeare Street, Southport, Merseyside PR8 5AB). Vicki has concentrated on Spain, gathering videotaped evidence of some of their crueller "animal sports". FAACE's report for 1993 made horrifying reading, but its work in publicising what is happening, has clearly had an effect. The 1994 report instanced several cases of massive fines against villages around Madrid which have ignored injunctions or regulations which are now being enforced. However, as Vicki Moore says, "We can't register as a charity, because the Charity Commission says our aim of intelligent legislation for animal welfare is political." No doubt, if FAACE confined itself to feeding the animals before they are tortured to death, our Charity Commission would be happy to deem it as "charitable".*

The Moore family consists of two humans, Miss Susie Dog, and four feline enchantresses. Victoria, black dress suit, white bib, sleek, velvety, jade oriental eyes, arrived as a tiny kitten who could fit with room to spare on the palm of the hand. Rescued from a winter stream, sole survivor of a litter deliberately drowned by persons unknown, Victoria possesses impeccable manners. She never scales vulnerable human flesh with extended claws, but taps on knees and requests to be lifted for cuddles.

Fleur Purr: black and white, with soft cotton wool fur and a highwayman mask. Although spayed at six months, Fleur's maternal instinct is overwhelming: she is little mother to everyone, animal or human. If we are ill, she takes up her position on the pillows and plays nurse. Fleur was rescued as a kitten: she was found trapped in a bag, suspended over a busy railway line.

Pepi, an elderly tabby lady, peppery by nature, spiritual daughter of the late Colonel Percy, a lovable striped curmudgeon, who spent his last years with us. Before she adopted us, Pepi tenanted a coal bunker.

Alita, la española, our Spanish cat, fiery, adorable, a fluffy, glorious riot of colour, red, gold, apricot, black and white, minus half a tail. As a three week old almost transparent wisp of a kitten on a Spanish street, her face was burnt with cigarettes, and her tail hacked off: I rescued her. The tiny kitten that went into quarantine on arrival in England, emerged six months later an elegant young cat, bemused and indignant by her enforced 'porridge'. Bi-national now, she retains a liking for garlic, calamari and gambas.

The two Victorias cuddle each other; Fleur looks on jealously from behind; Pepi looks affronted in front, and Alita has found such a comfortable cushion, she couldn't care less about the rest of them.

GERALD WELLS

Gerald Wells is proprietor of the National Wireless Museum, in West Norwood, South London, which has what must be the finest collection of early wirelesses in the country. It was featured on Tim Hunkin's The Secret Life of the Radio.

The Museum is open by appointment only: tel. 0181-670 3667.

Pushkin, a light tabby, is the archetypal stable-cat: so-called, because this kind of cat often hung around the stables and kept the horses company. She is an "A-reg", i.e. vintage 1984, and came as a rescue from a lady in Streatham who looks after stray or unwanted cats.

We get quite a lot of visits from women's guilds or church guilds. Many are not quite sure what they are coming to: they forget we are partly about the history of design. So if they're a bit on edge, Pushkin comes in through the door and immediately melts the ice. She is particularly good with small children, who then have something to look at and play with, if they are not so interested in the wireless.

Like most cats, Pushkin is quite geared in to food. When she is impatient for it, she jumps up on the side, and starts gnawing at the notices on the wall. Her next trick is to tap one or two cups hanging on the side-board: her bashes get stronger until I know I either have to accept an unnecessary breakage, or give in and feed her! Some friends in Aylesbury always bring special food for her when they visit. She now recognises the sound of their engine, and always emerges to greet them.

MICHAEL PARKIN

Michael Parkin is owner of the Michael Parkin Gallery in Belgravia. There, he concentrates on showing the work of 19th and 20th century British artists, from Whistler to Ben Nicholson. He is also a great collector of the best-known cat artist Louis Wain, and has an exhibition each Christmas called "Cats of Fame and Promise". His book Louis Wain's Cats, *first published in 1983, is still in print eleven years later. It is dedicated "To my four cats: Fortnum, Mason, Sarah and Sophie". The first two are now deceased; the latter two are still very much alive: not so surprising, as they are actually two of Michael's three daughters.*

My two previous cats, Fortnum and Mason, now lie in the garden under an imposing tombstone, with lettering designed by Eric Gill. Their replacements are Gainsborough, a British Blue boy, who thus gets his name from Gainsborough's picture "Blue Boy". Zoffany was our other great 18th century painter, so Gainsborough's female companion had to be Mrs Zoffany. She is a non-pedigree relation of Fortnum with very little of his aristocratic Persian breeding left, being a Tabby. She is nonetheless much loved, especially by Zuleika, my five-year-old daughter, who adores them both.

One cannot be too careful when choosing cats' names: two other cats I had were called Lytton, after Lytton Strachey, and Carrington, after Lytton's devoted admirer Dora Carrington. When Lytton (the cat) got run over, poor Carrington simply pined away: rather as Dora Carrington did in the human world. Mason proved a bit more robust when Fortnum went: but he too has now joined the Great Cat in the Sky.

Other cats in my life have included "Whisky", a Persian who used up one of his nine lives being blown across the garden when a flying bomb landed in 1944, and Mr Hodge (named after Dr. Johnson's cat), who used up all of his lives by being eaten by a bull terrior called "Bill Sykes" in the 1960s.

Opposite: Michael Parkin holds Gainsborough, while Zuleika holds Mrs Zoffany.

OTHER CELEBRITY CATS

This book was compiled by the author writing to all of those featured earlier, and to almost all of those mentioned below. Of course, all of them are busy people, and most had to be approached via their agents, which might explain why many did not reply. We have therefore derived much of the following information from published sources elsewhere, and apologise if it contains any inaccuracies. If any of those mentioned would now like to correct or amplify the information given, we should be happy to take this into account in a future edition.

Having featured two thriller writers earlier, we cannot fail to mention a third: P D James, or Baroness James of Holland Park, as she now is. Her secretary tells us that a few years ago, Lady James had two mischievous and lively Burmese called Pansy and Gilbert. Sadly, one after the other, they were stolen, but shortly afterwards Lady James was 'adopted' by a very beautiful white Persian stray with golden eyes, whom she called Hodge, after Dr Johnson's cat. When she first appeared, Hodge was in a bedraggled and highly nervous state and had obviously been living rough for some time. She has now been with Lady James for about five years and is deeply affectionate, happy, healthy and well-groomed.

Adopting a favourite feline practice of climbing even higher up the tree, we can mention two royal cats: those belonging to Princess Michael of Kent, and living in regal splendour in Kensington Palace. Princess Michael feels there has been too much publicity about her cats: an understandable feeling, when two of her cats were mauled to death last year by a mystery animal. She still has at least two cats, one of which is a Burmese called Mimi. (Could the other be called Rodolfo?)

TV presenters seem to have a remarkable variety of names for their cats. Fiona Armstrong has a splendid-looking large cat, completely black, called Max. Tim Brooke-Taylor, formerly of "The Goodies" but now in charge of BBC Radio Comedy, has a cat called Muriel. Keith Chegwin can boast no less than five cats, though only two names are recorded: Pooh Cat, and Goliath. Goliath must be named from his size; one hopes the former was named after Winnie the Pooh. Russell Grant the astrologer calls his cat Tamarisk: one wonders which sign she was born under?

Another TV personality with a cat is Julia Somerville. Her cat, Billy the Burmese, is really jointly owned, because when she goes off to read the news, Billy transfers his attentions to Julia's neighbour, the pianist Imogen Cooper, and stays in her place until Julia's return.

Talking of musicians, the soprano Kiri te Kanawa has two cats, called Flinty and Shady, at her Surrey home. But, as she told *Radio Times,* "We love them, but they'll be our last because I can't bear them destroying the local wildlife - the coots, ducks and robins. Magpies are killing enough birds without our cats joining in." No doubt she finds it upsetting constantly to find trophies of her cats' bird-hunting placed lovingly on the sitting-room carpet. Indeed, many cat-lovers must have asked themselves why such beautiful creatures end up behaving so barbarically? Instinct, one fears, is the true and simple answer.

Dame Kiri te Kanawa with one of her two cats. (Photo: Scope Features)

Howard Stableford, from Tomorrow's World, used to have no less than five cats: Preston, Ballou, Tex, Casey and Cisco. However, in his conservatory he keeps the ashes of two who were run over: Casey and Cisco. Keeping them there, rather than burying them in the garden, is an unusual idea, though as Howard's wife says, "We liked the idea of them continuing to stay with us."

Even those with a splendidly macho image are not immune to the attractions of a cat. Frank Bruno the boxer, for example, has two Siamese cats called Samson and Del Boy. As he told the *Mail on Sunday*, "They're very good-tempered, silky and loose. Sometimes they influence the way I move in the ring: they're so flexible." Only one politician is reported as having a cat: Giles Brandreth, MP, whose cat is called GB. One would like to think it was named after Brandreth's sphere of influence: Great Britain, but another explanation is more likely. The dress designer Elizabeth Emanuel has two cats, called Polo and Poser. Polo is a spotlessly white chinchilla - "a sort of James Bond cat", she says, while Poser is a slightly greyer Persian.

It is when we come to actors and actresses that we find a profusion of cats. The prize must undoubtedly be given to Tom Baker, who has no less than 17 of them. Only three names are recorded: Oscar, Dombey and Florence. These must attest to Tom Baker's literary interests: Oscar Wilde, of course, and Dombey and his sister Florence are the two principal characters in Dickens's *Dombey and Son*. Tom is also unusual (or should one say far-sighted?) by having already bought his gravestone - an old, second-hand one, one should add - and having it carefully carved "Tom Baker 1934 --". But if for himself, why not for his 17 cats too? Always assuming there are enough second-hand tombstones to spare ....

Next in the cat numbers game comes Leslie Phillips, who has five cats. Three of them came from Spain, and one is called Charles Claw. (We still await a gripping horror film about a rogue cat called Claws. Meantime, we must make do with an exhibition of that name in Newcastle: see page 46.) Dame Judi Dench and her husband Michael Williams have three cats plus a visitor. The first is called Newspapers (or Newps for short: does he collect the newspapers from the front door?): he is orange and white, with a Roman nose and flat feet. The second, Spider, is a black part-Burmese, while her son rejoices in the delightful name of Tobias Troutbeck. He is a spotted and striped oriental-looking Tabby, hence his nickname of "Tabs". No such pretensions for the visiting farm cat, Pushkin, who is tabby and white.

Frances de la Tour has two cats, Fluff and Snuggles, named by her children. In the kitchen is a large round table, on one side of which will be Frances doing paperwork, while on the other side will be her two children, Josh and Tommy, doing their homework. The cats' favourite place is sitting in the middle of the table between them. After all, where better can one get stroked by the entire family? Anna Carteret has a cat called Michael Jackson. This perhaps shows the pitfalls involved in naming one's cat after a celebrity. It is not known whether she now intends to get him a companion, to be called Lisa-Marie.

Sir Roy Strong (see page 12) in his magnificent garden in Herefordshire. (Photo: Scope Pictures)

Beryl Reid is well-known for her love of cats, as shown by her book *The Cat's Whiskers* (Headline paperback 1987), in which she described her cats. At that time, she had ten, of which five were ginger. The eldest was named Ronnie, after Ronnie Corbett, Clive, named after Clive Francis, Paris, after the God of Love, Billy and Tufnell. Also a tortoiseshell Elsie, and a tabby called Sir Harry, named after Harry Secombe, of course. Dimly was named when two friends of Beryl's asked where she was; one looked outside and then said, "I can just see her moving dimly". Sir Harry Secombe himself has a cat: named Moriarty after the character in the Goon Show, no doubt.

Beryl also writes about her actress friends: Eileen Atkins, who has three tabbies, Archie, Gus and Finnegan, while Sian Phillips has three Burmese: Spencer, because he looks rather grand, and two others called Barnaby and Rupert. Another actress with three Burmese is Hayley Mills: she keeps them down at her house at Hampton Court.

Some celebrities own both dogs and cats. The novelist Jilly Cooper, for example, is said to have between one and five cats: what she once described as a "floating population of cats". One is (or was) called Sewage.

The actress Jill Gascoine's cat is called Dodger: presumably after the Artful Dodger in *Oliver Twist:* so Dickens strikes again. Martin Shaw's cat is called Korky, which must take its name from the cartoon character. Nerys Hughes has two cats, obtained from an RSPCA cattery. Both were named by her children, and are called Cuddles and Twm Twm (Welsh for Tom Tom). The second name is in memory of another cat owned by her aunt in Wales.

Lastly, one can note that the commonest names for cats in Britain are names like Tabby or Tigger, Blacky or Sooty, and, of course, Puss. Not one of the celebrities' cats mentioned in this book are called by any of these names. Instead, almost all their names are both original and inventive. But then, perhaps people who are completely conventional are not so likely to be celebrities!

Ruth Rendell's Blanche (p. 14) does not like being disturbed.

Colonel Chinstrap (p. 28) finds a comfortable sleeping-place.

Gerald Wells' cat Pushkin (p. 34) draws attention to her need for breakfast.

CATS FEATURED

CELEBRITIES FEATURED

Eileen Atkins 42

Fiona Armstrong 38

Tom Baker 40

Richard Bawden 24

Giles Brandreth 38

Tim Brooke-Taylor 38

Frank Bruno 40

Bunny Campione 26

Anna Carteret 40

Keith Chegwin 38

Imogen Cooper 40

Jilly Cooper 42

Dame Judi Dench 40

Elizabeth Emanuel 42

Lady Fairbairn 28

Celia Fremlin 16

Jill Gascoine 42

Russell Grant 38

Molly Hardwick 22

Nerys Hughes 42

P D James 38

Dame Kiri te Kanawa 40

Francis King 18

Carla Lane 20

Josie Lawrence 10

Princess Michael of Kent 38

Hayley Mills 42

Victoria Moore 32

Erna Naughton 30

Michael Parkin 36

Leslie Phillips 40

Sian Phillips 42

Ruth Rendell 14

Beryl Reid 42

Sir Harry Secombe 42

Martin Shaw 42

Valerie Singleton 8

Julia Somerville 40

Howard Stableford 38

Sir Roy Strong 12

Frances de la Tour 40

Gerald Wells 34

Michael Williams 40

CLAWS!

FROM SABRETOOTHS TO SIAMESE

26 July 94 to 5 Feb 95

HANCOCK MUSEUM

Barras Bridge, Newcastle upon Tyne. Tel: **091 222 7418.**

Open: Mon-Sat 10am-5pm • Sun 2-5pm

Near Haymarket Metro

ADMISSION

£1.80 adults • £1.00 children 4-16yrs & concs • £5.50 family ticket

Metro

TWM TYNE & WEAR MUSEUMS

Printed on recycled paper

Other publications by Nicholas Reed, BA (Oxon), MA (Manc), MPhil (St.A.)

available from Lilburne Press:

Camille Pissarro at Crystal Palace (1987, rev. 1993)

Pissarro in West London (1990)

Pissarro in Essex (1992)

Sisley and the Thames (1991, rev. 1992)

Richmond and Kew Green (1992)

Four Generations of the Pissarro Family,

by K. Erickson and N. Reed (1993)

THE AUTHOR

Nicholas Reed, who acquired three degrees in classics and Roman archaeology, now specialises in placing artists, particularly the Impressionists, in their local context. In addition to his four books on the Impressionists in England, he also takes tours of places where the Impressionists painted around the outskirts of Paris. He is a lecturer for the National Association of Decorative and Fine Arts Societies.

In his spare time during the 1980s he founded and chaired both the Friends of Shakespeare's Globe, and the Friends of West Norwood Cemetery. Though he has never been active in organisations concerned with animals, he is a Life Member of the League Against Cruel Sports. Nicholas writes:

My cat Ajax was rescued from a housing co-operative where he was being treated badly. He is now very happy in his new home, where he has been for ten years. His greatest delight is being taken for a walk around the neighbouring streets, and indeed gets rather cross when I am too preoccupied to take him outside. Otherwise, he likes to spend his time trying to outstare the neighbouring black cat Oscar, and most recently has started muscling up to the neighbourhood visiting fox. A lot of spitting resulted in a retreat by the fox. This says much for Ajax's fearlessness, like the Greek hero (not the toilet cleaner) after whom he is named. It says rather less for his grasp of urban ecology.